JED PASCOE'S THE FUNNY SIDE OF Golf

THE AUTHOR WOULD
LIKE TO THANK THE
FOLLOWING PEOPLE
FOR THEIR HELP
IN PRODUCING
THIS BOOK:

PAUL ASHWELL
COLIN CARLOW
JOHNNY HILLIARD
JOHN LAYCOCK
DAN FOOTE
BOB HOPE
AND
MY WIFE, DERYL

Price £2.99
ISBN 1 874125 21 X

First Published in Great Britain by
Powerfresh Limited

3 Gray Street
Northampton
England
NN1 3QQ

Telephone 0604 30996 Country Code 44
Facsimile 0604 21013

© August 1993 Jed Pascoe

FUNNY SIDE OF GOLF
ISBN 1 874125 21 X

Printed in Britain by Avalon Print Ltd., Northampton.

ORIGINS of GOLF

GOLF (pronounced goll-f, goff, goalf or goaf) originated in Scotland as the ritual hunting of a small, white furry creature called, surprisingly, the **GOLF**.

⊛ This quiet and timid animal, much prized for it's delicate hide, lived in holes in the ground on smooth patches of grass between sand dunes near the Scottish coast

⊛ Large teams of men...and women...

called 'Golfers' would hunt the 'Golf', using wooden sticks to beat the poor creature senseless once it was found, then dropping it into its burrow, thus flushing out the next 'Golf' which was then chased across the 'links'...and so on all day. The first person to claim 18 golfs' sunk became the 'winner', and was rewarded with copious amounts of ale and whisky until he, too, sank out of sight.

⊙ Although today's golf is more environmentally sound, these basic traditions are still kept alive today. ☺

...PLUS GREEN FEES, BALLS, DESIGNER SPORTSWEAR, ACCESSORIES, BOOKS AND TUITION...
TO THINK THAT I ONCE BELIEVED GOLF TO BE A RICH MAN'S GAME!!

Golfing Types

① THE SNOB

Belongs to several of the Best Clubs... rarely seen except at Black Tie functions...

owns a desperately expensive set of clubs (as in irons and woods) ..hardly uses any of them... just shows everyone the cheque stubs...

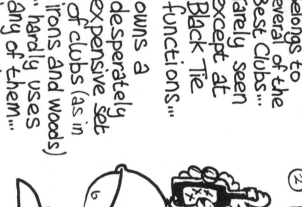

② THE SLOB

Cleans spike in hand basin of Gentlemen! washroom... Shows at leas 3" of bottom cleavage whils putting... embarrassing loud in the Bar.. handicap same as waist measurement...

③ THE IMMENSELY-RICH-BUT-TALENTLESS

Despite having the best equipment and tuition, he has a huge handicap; that is, he can't play golf to save his life... a great benefactor to his club... Plays with a gold-plated putter.. Pity his game isn't the same....

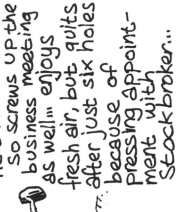

④ THE BUSINESS GOLFER

Attempts to combine business meetings with a 'quick round' but can't relax into his swing... a great competitor, he tries too hard.. so screws up the business meeting as well.. enjoys fresh air, but quits after just six holes because of pressing appointment with stockbroker...

⑤ THE KNOW-ALL

A crashing bore... tries to impress with his encyclo-paedic knowledge of the Game, its history, techniques, rules, and exponents from the year zero...

Quotes pre-war Championship tables.. always on hand with his opinion why your cherished and newly paid-for clubs aren't quite what he'd have bought...

⑥ THE NOVICE

Totally out of his depth... Came along because it loo[ks] like fun, whackin[g] balls around a beautifully cared-for green landscap[e] (good for stress you know?) Torn between thrashing with a driver or tapping around in just und[er] 200 with his 7 iro[n] (Basically, following example set by othe[r] on the course...")

① THE SATURDAY MORNING HACKER

Look out, Nicklaus! Here comes the Hacker! Buys balls by the grass... wears all the right clothes... and, believe it or not, plays for **fun!**

Thoroughly enjoys his game... can't wait to get his handicap out of three figures... can't wait to get into the Bar...

⑧ THE CUTTING EDGE

Buys all the <u>latest</u> clothes and gimmicks... uses <u>state-of-the-art</u> clubs (updated every six months)

noted for his collection of headgear... singlehandedly keeps the Pro-shop in business...

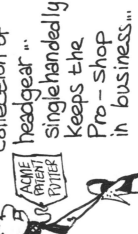

ACME
PATENT
PUTTER

9 THE TRADITIONAL

The polar opposite of the 'Cutting Edge'... this fellah learned his golf at his father's knee, as did his father before him... and he still uses the original clubs which aren't carbon-shafted as carbon — dated...

So much

10 THE RETIRED-BUT— DEDICATED

Honorary life member... plays a minimum of four rounds a week when most of his contempo- raries are getting fitted for Zimmer frames... has an annoying low teens handicap... once played in the same tournament as Bob Hope and Ben Hogan... "But," he says "There was a war on..."

⑫ THE LEFT-HANDER

Damn awkward to play against... Seems to do everything backwards...

But don't laugh if he shanks... he may be Henry Cooper...

⑪ THE WEE CANNY SCOT

Plays with a motley collection of clubs, ranging from gleaming mahogany and maple matched woods (which on a good day can ace any hole under 350 yards) to an ancient mashie (it still has it's uses, ye ken...). Don't be fooled into gambling with this man... his country invented the game...

⑬ THE COLONEL

Ex-Indian Army... ex-cavalry... treats Clubhouse as a substitute Officer's Mess... Hrrumphs and Hurrs if a member wears a gaudy tie... a born Chairman, he organises the people who organise everything else... low handicap... thinks of 'gaff' as polo without the horse...

⑭ THE AM-CHAMP

A certain flair on the fairway... A knack of returning a birdie off a 475-yard dog-leg... without batting an eyelid... good-humoured, helpful, modest, lethal... would have turned pro but couldn't spare the time from the ice-hockey and chess...

MY HUSBAND
THINKS I'M
SEEING
ANOTHER MAN...

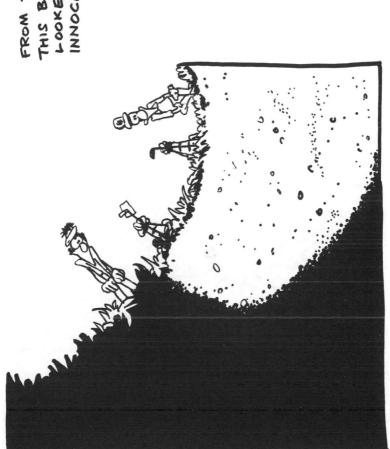

FROM THE TEE, THIS BUNKER LOOKED QUITE INNOCENT...

THE MYSTERY
OF THE
LOST BALL

NO'' NOT THE 19TH HOLE ''' THE 13TH, 14TH AND DOGLEG 16TH'''

UNEXPECTED HAZARDS OF EXOTIC, FOREIGN COURSES...

IMAGINE McCRAGGAN'S IRRITATION WHEN, WITHOUT WARNING, THE WEE SASSENACH COMMENCED WHISTLING 'SCOTLAND THE BRAVE' DURING A CRUCIAL BIRDIE PUTT...

VISITORS SEARCHING FOR THE NEXT TEE ON AN UNFAMILIAR COURSE...

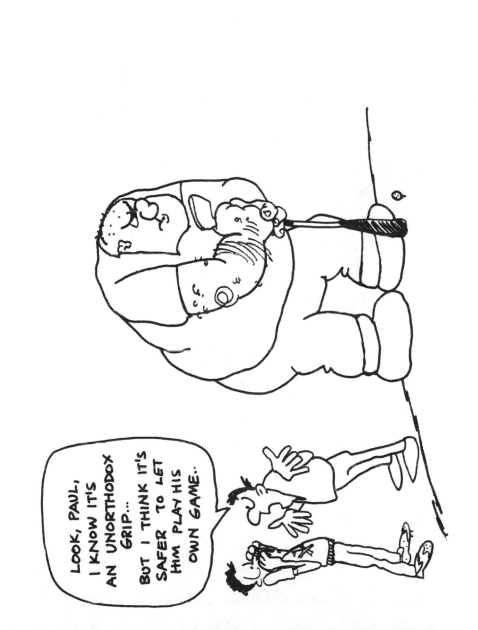

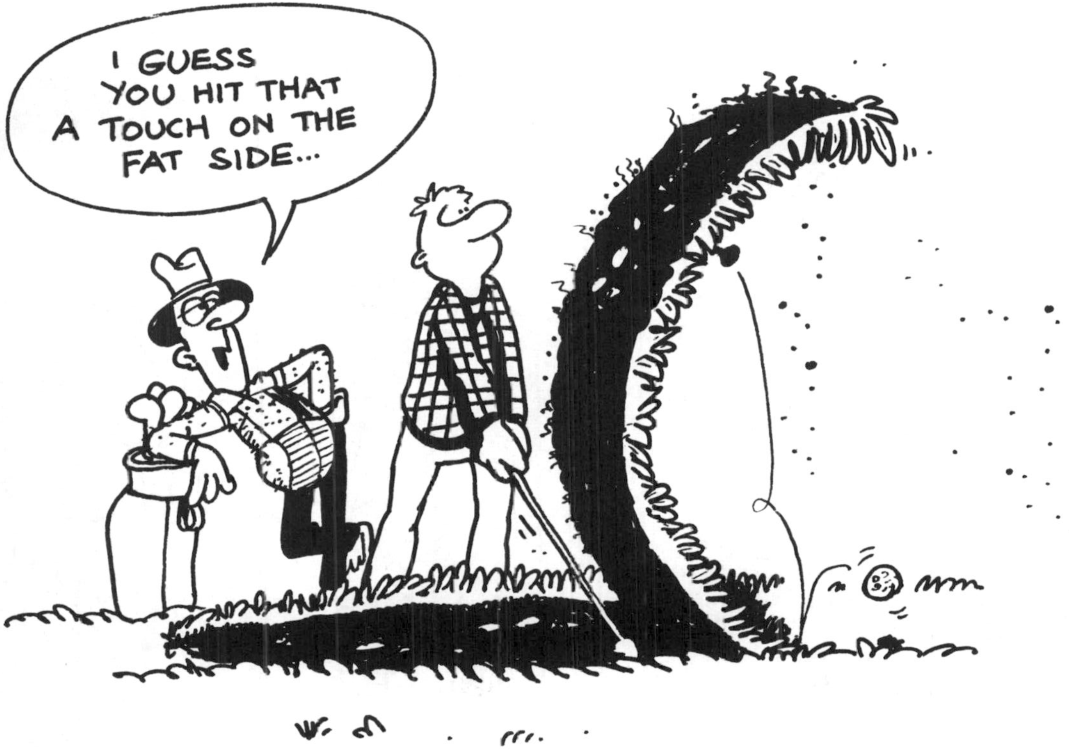
I GUESS YOU HIT THAT A TOUCH ON THE FAT SIDE...

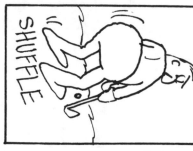

WIGGLE
WIGGLE

SHUFFLE

PRACTICE
WHISK

SHUFFLE
WIGGLE
WHISK
WHISK
WIGGLE

SHUFFLE

FINAL
SPTAK!

IT TAKES
A LOT OF
SETTING
UP TO
TOP THEM
AS BADLY
AS THAT...!

A MOST EMBARRASSING MOMENT:

EXCUSE ME,
YOUNG MAN...
BUT DO YOU MIND
IF THE LADIES'
KNITTING CIRCLE
PLAYS THROUGH?

No Bull Dept.

WE SEND THE DIVERS INTO THE LAKE TWICE A YEAR... LAST TIME, THEY CAME OUT WITH 7,000 BALLS!

"THE COURSES IN THIS PART OF ARIZONA WERE PARTICULARLY TESTING."

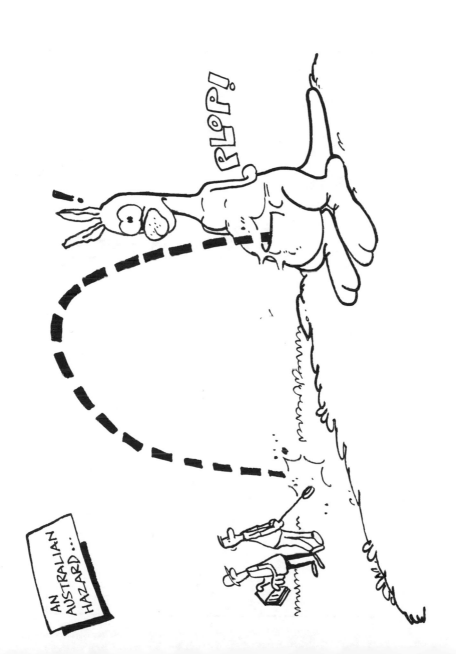

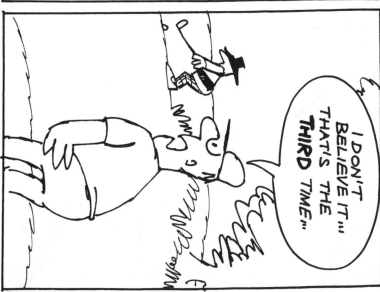

STANDARD'S DOWN ON LAST YEAR, WILSON...

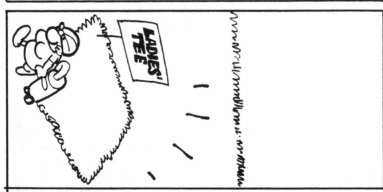

THE COMMITTEE REQUESTS THAT YOU CONFINE YOUR DEMONSTRATIONS TO THE PRACTICE RANGE !!!

A CAUTIONARY TALE ...

THE MEMBERS TOOK PAINS TO POINT OUT THAT THE VISITOR'S CAR PARK WAS ON THE **LEFT**-HAND SIDE OF THE ROAD!!!

Price £2.99

ISBN 1 874125 21 X

First Published in Great Britain by
Powerfresh Limited
3 Gray Street
Northampton
England
NN1 3QQ

Telephone 0604 30996 Country Code 44
Facsimile 0604 21013

© August 1993 Jed Pascoe

FUNNY SIDE OF GOLF
ISBN 1 874125 21 X

Printed in Britain by Avalon Print Ltd., Northampton.

JED PASCOE
NATIONAL AND INTERNATIONAL
AWARD WINNING
CARTOONIST.
LIVING PROOF THAT
EMPTY VESSELS MAKE
MOST NOISE..
TOTALLY CONFUSED BY
LIFE, HE LIVES MAINLY
IN HIS BELEAGURED
IMAGINATION—WHICH
IS ENOUGH TO
CONFUSE ANYONE. AND
STILL LOOKING FOR FAME
AND FORTUNE, IF ANYONE
OUT THERE IS INTERESTED.